Front Cover: 37418, once named *East Lancashire Railway*, entered preservation with the East Lancashire Railway where it is noted stabled in Baron Street yard on 6 January 2012.

Rear Cover: 37430 *Cwmbran* + 37412 *Driver George Elliot* bear Transrail Freight livery and branding as they stable at Southport on 25 April 1999 with the stock of a Southport–Edinburgh charter that had run the previous day.

THE ENGLISH ELECTRIC CLASS 37/4 DIESEL LOCOMOTIVES

FRED KERR

PEN & SWORD TRANSPORT

AN IMPRINT OF PEN & SWORD BOOKS LTD
YORKSHIRE – PHILADELPHIA

First published in Great Britain in 2022 by
Pen and Sword Transport
An imprint of
Pen & Sword Books Ltd.
Yorkshire – Philadelphia

ISBN 978 1 39909 613 3

Typeset in 10/12 Palatino by SJmagic DESIGN SERVICES, India.

Printed and bound by Printworks Global Ltd, London/Hong Kong.

Pen & Sword Books Ltd incorporates the imprints of Pen & Sword Books Archaeology, Atlas, Aviation, Battleground,
Discovery, Family History, History, Maritime, Military, Naval, Politics, Railways, Select, Transport, True Crime, Fiction,
Frontline Books, Leo Cooper, Praetorian Press, Seaforth Publishing, Wharncliffe and White Owl.

For a complete list of Pen & Sword titles please contact

PEN & SWORD BOOKS LIMITED
47 Church Street, Barnsley, South Yorkshire, S70 2AS, England
E-mail: enquiries@pen-and-sword.co.uk
Website: www.pen-and-sword.co.uk

or

PEN AND SWORD BOOKS
1950 Lawrence Rd, Havertown, PA 19083, USA
E-mail: Uspen-and-sword@casematepublishers.com
Website: www.penandswordbooks.com

CONTENTS

ABBREVIATIONS

BR	British Railways/Rail
C&W	Carriage & Wagon
CS	Carriage Sidings
ecs	empty coaching stock
DB	Deutsches Bundesbahn
DBS	DB Schenker
DMU	Diesel Multiple Unit
DRS	Direct Rail Services
ETH	Electric Train Heating
EWS	English Welsh & Scottish
EWSR	English Welsh & Scottish Railways
FoSCL	Friends of the Settle & Carlisle Line
IECC	Integrated Electronic Control Centre
NRM	National Rail Museum
RC&W	Railway Carriage & Wagon
RfD	Railfreight Distribution
RTC	Research Technical Centre
SRPS	Scottish Railway Preservation Society
T&RSMD	Traction & Rolling Stock Maintenance Depot
TSS	Twin Screw Ship
WCRC	West Coast Railway Company

CLASS 37/4 – THE MIXED TRAFFIC MARVEL

by Fred Kerr

When British Railways introduced its Pilot Scheme in 1955, it initially identified three power ranges for its main line fleet – Type A = 800-1000 hp, Type B = 1000-1499 hp and Type C = 2000+ hp. It soon became apparent that the 1500-2000 hp range offered a more suitable power range for mixed traffic duties and a specification was issued that led to three designs being ordered from Birmingham RC&W (later Class 33), Beyer Peacock (later Class 35) and English Electric (later Class 37).

Over time the Class 37 design proved its worth, with 309 locomotives being ordered and delivered between December 1960 thru January 1966, but in the early 1980s thoughts turned to replacing them after twenty years' service. A specification for a replacement Type 3 design, designated Class 38, was mooted, but this was cancelled as part of the policy that saw a hundred Class 60 freight locomotives being ordered and a refurbishment programme being initiated for a number of Class 37 locomotives on behalf of service sectors.

The refurbishment coincided with the division of British Railways into sectors and the sector for secondary/local passenger services, Provincial Railways, identified a need for thirty-one locomotives to be fitted with Electric Train Heat (ETH). These were intended for operation in Scotland on both the West Highland Line and Far North services north of Inverness and the Welsh Marches Line between Crewe and Cardiff. Class doyen 37401 entered traffic in June 1985; the remaining conversions were delivered between then and that of 37431 in January 1986. Once introduced to service, the fleet was divided between three depots: 37401 - 413 / 422 - 425 to (Glasgow) Eastfield for West Highland Line services, 37414 - 421 to Inverness for Far North services, and 37426 - 431 to Cardiff for Cambrian Line services.

As class members were released from passenger duty by the introduction of new 'Sprinter' trainsets, many were transferred to freight duty and often received the sector livery of the new operator. When BR was privatised from 1 April 1994, replete with a new structure suitable for franchising (passenger services) or selling (freight services), the fleet was allocated to Transrail Freight – the freight company serving the North West of England and Scotland.

The three main freight companies (Loadhaul, Mainline Freight and Transrail Freight) were bought by the American Wisconsin Central Railway company in February 1996 and melded into a unified company that operated as English, Welsh, Scottish Railways (EWSR), hence the locomotives still remained with a single operator. The fleet continued to be operated by EWSR but withdrawals from service, either to be used as spares or sold into preservation, reduced the fleet until 2010 when EWSR, by then operating as DB Schenker (DBS), withdrew the survivors from service and offered them for sale.

The surviving fleet was bought by Direct Rail Services (DRS), based at Carlisle to service the transport needs of the nuclear industry geared to Sellafield, initially to haul the nuclear flasks, but the presence of the ETH equipment has seen the class remaining on passenger duties. The influx of new DMU fleets during 2020 has seen this work diminish and a fleet review is expected to see further class withdrawals in the near future.

Since the introduction of the Class 37/4 fleet in June 1985, class members have undertaken a wide variety of services throughout the country and this album is dedicated to the various workings that have been photographed by me; not all services have been photographed but enough have been included in this album to confirm the reason why, after thirty-five years of service since refurbishment, the Class 37/4 contribution to the Class 37 history has also contributed to the class epithet as 'The Mixed Traffic Marvel'.

@ Fred Kerr June 2022

SECTION 1: SCOTLAND

The main beneficiary of the new fleet was the Scottish Region which received twenty-five locomotives to operate on two main routes: seventeen locomotives (37401 - 413; 37422 - 425) based at (Glasgow) Eastfield to work on the West Highland services between Glasgow and Mallaig and eight locomotives (37414 - 421) based at Inverness to work on the Far North services between Inverness and Kyle of Lochalsh/Thurso/Wick. Most of the duties were on passenger services, hence the introduction of the Class 156 / 158 Sprinter fleets during the early 1990s saw many of the locomotives being replaced and transferred to England where they were used on a variety of services – both freight and passenger.

The West Highland Line, however, requires diesel locomotives to power the sleeper service to/from Euston between Glasgow Queen St (later Edinburgh) and Fort William hence the use of Class 37/4 locomotives remained until more modern locomotives, in the guise of Class 67, became available from June 2006.

Left (Image 1): 37424 *Glendarroch* stables at Fort William depot on 31 August 1988 while awaiting its next duty.

Below (Image 2): 37403 *Isle of Mull* stables at Fort William depot on 29 August 1988 while awaiting its next duty.

Above (Image 3):
37410 *Aluminium 100* stables at Oban platform on 29 August 1988 awaiting its next duty.

Right (Image 4):
37412 *Loch Lomond* enters Spean Bridge on 2 September 1988 while working the Glasgow Queen St–Fort William service that includes the sleeping car portion from Euston.

(Image 5): 37425 *Sir Robert McAlpine/Concrete Bob* climbs to Spean Bridge on 27 August 1988 while working a Fort William–Glasgow Queen St service that included the overnight sleeper coaches for London Euston.

In 1988 the Provincial Railways sector introduced its Mainline livery, based on that adopted by the Inter City sector for its locomotive fleet and demonstrated it on West Highland Line services during August 1988. The first recipient was 37401, which was also named *Mary Queen of Scots*, to continue the Scottish themes that the West Highland Line fleet of Class 37/4 locomotives sought to promulgate.

(Image 6): 37401 *Mary Queen of Scots* awaits departure from Fort William on 28 August 1988 while working a Glasgow Queen St–Mallaig service that had been operated to publicise the new Mainline livery.

At the beginning of the 21st Century the only regular working of Class 37/4 traction on the West Highland Line were locomotives hired from EWSR to power the overnight sleeper service from London Euston and the seasonal *Royal Scotsman* tour programme operated by a private company. The Scottish Railway Preservation Society (SRPS) had also begun a charter programme from the Edinburgh/Glasgow area that was based on visits to Fort William and Mallaig, hence also required Class 37 traction, given the operating restrictions placed on other locomotive classes traversing the route.

(Image 7): 37427 bears EWSR livery and branding as it departs from Fort William on 31 August 2002 while working a Fort William–Edinburgh service that includes the overnight sleeping coaches for London Euston.

(Image 8): 37427 enters Spean Bridge on 25 August 2002 while working an Edinburgh–Fort William service that includes the overnight sleeper coaches from London Euston.

(Image 9): Having arrived at Fort William on 31 August 2002 with the morning service from Edinburgh, that included the sleeper coaches from London Euston, 37427 was used to pilot sister engine 37428 between Fort William and Mallaig when the latter arrived at Fort William while working a Scottish Railway Preservation Society charter from Ayr to Mallaig. The duo are noted crossing the swing bridge at Banavie under the shadow of Ben Nevis while on the outward journey.

The *Royal Scotsman* is a private company, initially operated by The Great Scottish & Western Railway Company, that organised a rail tour programme within Scotland geared to the American market. It began operating in 1985 but was acquired by Oriental Hotels (owners of the Venice-Simplon Orient Group) in 2005 after which the haulage contract was awarded to the West Coast Railway Company (WCRC) based at Carnforth in Lancashire. The Orient Hotels Group was bought by Belmond Group in 2014 and the latter company still operates the service as at 2020.

Class 37/4 traction hauled the *Royal Scotsman* trains up to 2005 and in April 1995 EWSR arranged to re-paint 37428 into a livery matching the *Royal Scotsman* stock; later additions to the West Highland Line locomotive pool were similarly treated with 37401 being repainted in March 2001 and 37416 being re-painted in April 2004.

Above (Image 10): The crest of The Great Scottish & Western Railway Company as applied to the dedicated locomotives.

Right (Image 11)/Below (Image 12): 37401 *The Royal Scotsman* approaches Rannoch on 26 May 2005 while working the Edinburgh–Fort William service that includes the Euston–Fort William portion of the overnight 'Highlander' sleeper service from London.

Above left (Image 13): The driver of 37401 *The Royal Scotsman* waits for the signal to detach the lounge cars from the sleeper coaches at Edinburgh Waverley after arriving from Fort William in the early hours of 17 May 2005. Once the shunt moves had been completed, 37401 *The Royal Scotsman* would continue to Millerhill depot to refuel before returning to Edinburgh Waverley to work the northbound sleeper service to Fort William.

Above right (Image 14): Resting from *Royal Scotsman* duties, 37428 *Loch Long/Loch Awe* stables at Fort William on 26 August 2002 while on overnight sleeper duties between Fort William and Edinburgh.

Below (Image 15): 37428 *Loch Long/Loch Awe* eases into Spean Bridge on 31 August 2002 while working an SRPS charter from Ayr to Mallaig.

(Image 16): Shortly after gaining the *Royal Scotsman* haulage contract, WCRC Class 37/0 37261 pilots Class 31/1 31190 *Gryphon* through Ardlui on 20 June 2005 while working the Taynuilt–Wemyss Bay leg of the *Royal Scotsman* tour as 37401 *The Royal Scotsman* waits to enter the single track section while working the Edinburgh–Fort William service that includes the Fort William portion of the overnight 'Highlander' sleeper service from London Euston.

(Image 17): 37416 awaits departure from Edinburgh Waverley in the early hours of 8 April 2005 while working the Edinburgh–Fort William service that includes the Fort William portion of the 'Highlander' sleeper service from London Euston.

(Image 18): 37428 *Loch Long/Loch Awe* accelerates out of Fort William on 26 August 2002 with the Fort William–Edinburgh service that includes the Fort William portion of the overnight southbound 'Highlander' sleeper service to London Euston.

SECTION 2: ENGLAND

2.1: SOUTHPORT / BLACKPOOL CLUB TRAINS

Once displaced from Scottish Region service the Class 37/4 locomotives were transferred to England where many were allocated to one of the freight sectors that had been introduced in the early 1980s. In May 1991 Regional Railways, renamed from Provincial Railways in 1989, elected to re-introduce the dedicated Club Train services between Blackpool North/Southport and Manchester Victoria to alleviate the then shortage of multiple unit trainsets.

Regional Railways arranged the hire of locomotives from Railfreight Distribution (RfD) and created a pool comprising 37415 / 416 / 419 / 426 / 430 *Cwmbran*, all bearing Provincial Railways Mainline livery and nominally based at (Sheffield) Tinsley depot, to work the services which comprised a train from each centre to Manchester each weekday morning and returning from Manchester to each centre each weekday night. The first stage was to train crews at both Southport and Blackpool for which 37430 *Cwmbran* was allocated; crews were trained during May and June 1991 and the new timetable began from 8 July 1991.

The working of the Club Trains actually operated in three periods which were influenced by locomotive reliability : -
- May 1991 thru July 1992 using Class 37/4s until poor reliability, despite the replacement of 37430 *Cwmbran* by 37417 *Highland Region* in May 1992, led to the introduction of Class 31/4 traction.
- July 1992 thru March 1993 using Class 31/4s – initially in pairs – until poor reliability led to the restoration of Class 37/4 traction.
- 21 March 1993 when the appearance of 37414 announced the creation of a Crewe-based pool initially comprising 37414 / 425 / 429; these were joined by 37407 / 421 / 422 in May 1993, 37408 / 418 in June 1993 and 37402 in November 1993. In December 1994 37402 / 407 underwent overhaul and were replaced by 37405 / 420.

Southport was declared an unstaffed halt by Regional Railways North West from 16 January 1995 and the consequent operation of the Club Train, involving stock moves between Manchester and Southport, led to cessation of Southport services in May 1995.

(Image 19): 37430 *Cwmbran* bears Provincial Railways Mainline livery as it sets back into the platform at Southport on 17 May 1991 with the Club Train stock after reversing the trainset.

Scenes From the Driver Training Programme

Above left (Image 20): 37430 *Cwmbran* climbs out of Meols Cop on 5 June 1991 while working the 07:16 Southport–Manchester Victoria service as part of the driver training programme.

Above right (Image 21): 37430 *Cwmbran* passes Burscough Bridge signalbox on 3 June 1991 with the evening Manchester Victoria–Southport service that formed part of the driver training programme.

Below (Image 22): 37430 *Cwmbran* awaits departure from Burscough Bridge on 8 July 1991 (the first day of official Club Train operation) with the evening Manchester Victoria–Southport service.

(Image 23): After the arrival of the evening Club Train at Southport, the trainset was initially reversed through the carriage sidings to the buffer stop on the line which once served as the station avoiding line. The stock was then hauled forward onto the Southport–Liverpool electrified line before reversing back into Platform 3 from where it drew forward onto the Southport–Wigan line for a final reversal into platform 5 or 6 for overnight stabling. On 31 May 1991 37430 *Cwmbran* had reached the buffer stops during this reversal procedure and prepared to draw forward to the Southport–Liverpool line.

Meols Cop station was adjacent to the end of my street during the period of Club Train operation hence I photographed many of the morning departures from Meols Cop which was situated at the bottom of a steep climb out of Southport. Locomotives noted at work on this service included …

Above left (Image 24): … 37415 on 24 June 1992.

Above right (Image 25): … 37417 *Highland Region* on 6 July 1992. This was the final working by Class 37/4 traction before the introduction of Class 31/4 traction on the Club Trains; these began with the return working of the service from Manchester Victoria later that night.

Below (Image 26): … 37419 on 12 July 1991.

Above left (Image 27): 37417 *Highland Region* joins the Southport–Liverpool line on 29 June 1992 during the stock reversal manoeuvre.

Above right (Image 28): 37426 joins the Southport–Liverpool line on 17 June 1992 during the stock reversal manoeuvre.

Below (Image 29): 37415 reverses the Club Train stock into Southport's platform 3 on 2 September 1991 during the stock reversal procedure.

Above left (Image 30): 37417 *Highland Region* approaches Burscough Bridge on 15 June 1992 with the evening Club Train to Southport.

Above right (Image 31): 37419 pilots failed 37426 out of Meols Cop on 12 August 1991 while working the morning Club Train to Manchester Victoria.

Below (Image 32): 37430 *Cwmbran* curves into Southport on 8 August 1991 with the 09:50 Manchester Victoria–Southport dated service. This train was formed of the morning Blackpool North Club Train trainset which returned to Manchester Victoria as an empty stock service and assisted with locomotive changeovers between the two Club Train services.

Above (Image 33): 37416 climbs out of Meols Cop on 10 July 1991 while working a Southport–Manchester Victoria relief service running in conjunction with the Open Golf Championship being held at Hillside Golf Club.

Opposite above left (Image 34): The first sign of the new order came on 25 March 1993 when 37414 *Cathays C&W Works 1846-1993*, replete in the latest Regional Railways livery, powered out of Meols Cop while working the morning Club Train service to Manchester Victoria.

Opposite above right (Image 35): 37425 *Sir Robert McAlpine/Concrete Bob* still bears its Railfreight Construction sector livery and branding as it powers out of Meols Cop on 4 May 1993 with the morning Club Train service to Manchester Victoria.

Opposite below (Image 36): 37407 *Loch Long* still bears its Provincial Railways Mainline livery as it curves out of Southport on 18 May 1993 while working the morning Club Train service to Manchester Victoria.

The Southport/Blackpool North Club Trains returned to Class 37/4 haulage in March 1993 when Regional Railways created a pool of locomotives based at Crewe, nominally for infrastructure duties but used for both the Club Trains and North Wales Coast services (see **Section 3.2**).

The return coincided with the advent of privatisation (in April 1994) when sectorisation gave way to franchises and Train Operating Companies; the Class 37/4 fleet had been distributed among a number of freight sectors hence the appearance of a variety of liveries borne by the locomotives now part of the Crewe-based pool.

(Image 37): 37429, bearing Regional Railways livery, has yet to regain its *Eisteddfod Genedlaethol* nameplates as it powers out of Meols Cop on 30 June 1993 with the morning service to Manchester.

Scenes from Meols Cop of the morning Club Train to Manchester Victoria.

(Image 38): 37402 *Bont Y Bermo* bears Provincial Railways Mainline livery as it departs from Meols Cop on 31 May 1994.

(Image 39): 37408 *Loch Rannoch* bears original ScotRail large logo livery as it departs from Meols Cop on 22 June 1993.

(Image 40): 37418 *Pectinidae* bears Railfreight Petroleum sector livery and branding as it departs from Meols Cop on 24 June 1993.

With the introduction of the Integrated Electronic Control Centre (IECC) at Sandhills there was a change to the stock reversal procedure at Southport. The Club Train trainset was directed to Platform 6 then reversed into Bradford Siding where the locomotive ran round the trainset to reverse it back into Platform 6 for overnight stabling and servicing.

Left (Image 41): 37422 *Robert F Fairlie* bears Regional Railways livery as it stables in Bradford Siding on 19 March 1994 during the commissioning of the IECC.

Below (Image 42): 37422 *Robert F Fairlie* reverses the club train stock into Southport's platform 6 on 10 April 1994.

(Image 43): 37402 *Bont Y Bermo* carries de-branded Railfreight two-tone Grey livery as it stables overnight in Southport on 27 February 1995.

(Image 44): 37407 *Blackpool Tower* carries Transrail Freight livery as it stables overnight in Southport on 28 February 1995.

(Image 45): 37408 *Loch Rannoch* bears original ScotRail large logo livery as it reverses the Club Train stock into Bradford Siding on 29 March 1995.

(Image 46): 37414 *Cathays C&W Works 1846-1993* bears Regional Railways livery as it curves into Southport on 5 September 1994 while working the evening Club Train service from Manchester Victoria.

(Image 47): 37425 *Sir William McAlpine/ Concrete Bob* bears Railfreight Construction sector livery and branding as it reverses the Club Train stock into Bradford Siding on 5 July 1994.

Morning Club Train departures to Manchester Victoria from Meols Cop by locomotives bearing Regional Railways livery include …

(Image 48): … 37421 *The Kingsman* on 28 April 1994.

(Image 49): … 37422 *Robert F Fairlie* on 11 May 1993.

(Image 50): … 37418 *East Lancashire Railway* on 19 May 1994.

Above (Image 51): 37421 *The Kingsman* bears Regional Railways livery as it stables in Southport overnight on 9 January 1994.

Opposite above (Image 52): 37429 *Eisteddfod Genedlaethol* bears Regional Railways livery as it powers out of Meols Cop on 18 May 1994 while working the morning Club Train to Manchester Victoria.

Opposite below (Image 53): 37425 *Sir Robert McAlpine/Concrete Bob* bears Railfreight Construction sector livery and branding as it curves into St Lukes on 14 July 1994 while working the morning Club Train to Manchester Victoria.

(Image 54): When Regional Railways North West decreed that Southport would be operated as an unstaffed halt for its services from 16 January 1995, the Club Train diagrams changed to include ecs workings between Manchester and Southport. On 21 April 1995 37418 *East Lancashire Railway* passed Burscough Locks while en route to (Manchester) Longsight CS with the evening Club Train trainset for overnight maintenance and stabling..

(Image 55): 37429 *Eisteddfod Genedlaethol* approaches Pool Hey crossing on 12 May 1995 while working the Club Train trainset to (Manchester) Longsight CS for overnight maintenance and stabling.

(Image 56): 37418 *East Lancashire Railway* climbs out of Parbold on 22 April 1995 while working the morning Club Train from Southport to Manchester Victoria.

Arrival of the evening Club Train from Manchester Victoria at Southport with locomotives bearing Regional Railways livery include …

(Image 57): … 37418 *East Lancashire Railway* on 15 May 1995.

(Image 58): … 37429 *Eisteddfod Genedlaethol* on 12 May 1995.

Image 59): … 37421 *The Kingsman* on 26 April 1995.

(Image 60): The only train accident during the Club Train era occurred on 25 May 1995 when 37420 *The Scottish Hosteller*, bearing Provincial Railways Mainline livery, reversed the stock too far down the platform causing the rear coach to over-ride the buffer stop onto the concourse; hence the cancellation of that morning's service to Manchester Victoria.

(Image 61): 37421 *The Kingsman* curves out of Southport on 1 May 1995 while working the morning Club Train to Manchester Victoria.

(Image 62): 37422 *Robert F Fairlie* curves out of Southport on 2 May 1995 while working the morning Club Train to Manchester Victoria.

(Image 63): 37421 *The Kingsman* propels the Club Train trainset into Bradford Siding on 27 March 1995 before running round the trainset to propel it back into Southport's platform 6.

(Image 64): ***The End of an Era***. 37407 *Blackpool Tower,* bearing Transrail Freight livery and branding, curves out of Southport on 26 May 1995 with the final locomotive-hauled Southport–Manchester Victoria Club Train. The locomotive pool and trainsets were subsequently transferred to the North Wales Coast services (see **Section 3.2**)

The Club Train programme also included a service to Blackpool North which operated with the same traction pool as the Southport service. Scenes from the Blackpool North services include …

(Image 65): … 37429 *Eisteddfod Genedlaethol* calling at Salford Crescent on 22 May 1995 while working the evening Manchester Victoria–Blackpool North Club Train service.

(Image 66): … 37418 *East Lancashire Railway* speeding through Singleton on 19 April 1995 while working the evening Manchester Victoria–Blackpool North Club Train service.

(Image 67): … 37418 *East Lancashire Railway* standing at Blackpool North on 27 June 1995 after arriving with the Club Train from Manchester Victoria.

(Image 68): 37417 *Highland Region* bears Provincial Railways Mainline livery as it passes Bolton on 5 June 1992 while working a Blackpool North–Manchester Victoria Club Train stock move.

(Image 69): 37418 *East Lancashire Railway* enters Blackpool North on 27 June 1995 while working an evening Club Train service from Manchester Victoria.

(Image 70): … 37417 *Highland Region* bears Provincial Railways Mainline livery as it speeds through Farington on 27 June 1992 while working a Blackpool North–Liverpool Lime St service that sees the Club Train trainset transfer to Edge Hill CS for maintenance.

The Regional Railways North West franchise was awarded to First Group, operating as First North Western, that began on 2 March 1997. In 2000 the company elected to run a 'Farewell' tour over the North West routes over which Class 37/4 traction had operated.

Right (Image 71): 37421 + 37415, both bearing EWSR livery and branding, arrive at Southport from Crewe on 21 May 2000 to take over the next leg of the railtour from Class 37/0 37038 + 37029 which had earlier arrived with the Crewe–Southport leg of the 'Farewell' railtour. Note that 37415 bears original 'EW&S' branding whilst 37421 bears revised 'EWS' branding.

Below (Image 72): 37415 leads 37421 as they race through Bescar Lane on 21 May 2000 with the Southport–Manchester Victoria leg of the 'Farewell' railtour.

2.2: YORKSHIRE & SETTLE & CARLISLE

Arriva Northern Trains faced a train shortage during 2003 for which it hired 3 Class 37/4 locomotives, 37405 / 408 / 411, from freight operator EWSR to operate a number of diagrams covering Leeds–Knaresborough and Leeds–Carlisle services. The trainset comprised four coaches operated by a pair of locomotives working in top 'n tail mode and a further locomotive being retained as spare/maintenance; it began operating from September 2003 and continued until September 2004 when a new timetable was implemented.

(Image 73): 37408 *Loch Rannoch*, working in top 'n tail mode with 37411 *Scottish Railway Preservation Society*, curves off Ribblehead Viaduct on 3 July 2004 while working a Carlisle–York service.

(Image 74): 37405 is at the rear of a Healey Mills–Leeds stock move on 20 May 2004 as it curves out of Healey Mills behind 37411 *Scottish Railway Preservation Society*.

(Image 75): 37408 *Loch Rannoch* forms the rear of a Leeds–Carlisle service hauled by 37411 *Scottish Railway Preservation Society* while calling at Keighley on 3 December 2003.

(Image 76): 37408 *Loch Rannoch* works in top 'n tail mode with 37411 *Scottish Railway Preservation Society* as the consist approaches Long Preston on 24 July 2004 while working a Carlisle–Leeds service.

Above left (Image 77): 37408 *Loch Rannoch*, working in top 'n tail mode with 37411 *Scottish Railway Preservation Society*, speeds out of Blea Moor Tunnel on 5 May 2004 while working a Leeds–Carlisle service.

Above right (Image 78): 37408 *Loch Rannoch*, working in top 'n tail mode with 37411 *Scottish Railway Preservation Society*, nears the summit of Ais Gill on 5 May 2004 while working a Carlisle–Leeds service.

(Image 79): 37411 *Scottish Railway Preservation Society* works in top 'n tail mode with 37405 as it curves out of Healey Mills on 20 May 2004 while working a Healey Mills–Leeds stock move.

(Image 80): 37405 works in top 'n tail mode with 37411 *Scottish Railway Preservation Society* as it approaches Bolton Percy on 12 June 2004 while working a Knottingley–York stock move and …

(Image 81): … receives rear end assistance from 37411 *Scottish Railway Preservation Society*.

(Image 82): 37411 *Scottish Railway Preservation Society* works in top 'n tail mode with 37408 *Loch Rannoch* as they curve into Lazonby & Kirkoswald on 23 April 2004 while working a Carlisle–Leeds service.

(Image 83): 37411 *Scottish Railway Preservation Society* works in top 'n tail mode with 37408 *Loch Rannoch* as they approach Appleby on 10 September 2004 while working a Carlisle–Leeds service.

(Image 84): 37411 *Scottish Railway Preservation Society* works in top 'n tail mode with 37408 *Loch Rannoch* as they cross Dent Head viaduct on 23 April 2004 while working a Leeds–Carlisle service.

SECTION 3: WALES

3.1: CAMBRIAN LINES

The original intention had been to operate the Welsh fleet, 37426-431, on Marches services, but on introduction to service at Cardiff they were used on Cardiff–Bristol/Fishguard/Portsmouth services in addition to replacing Class 33 traction on Cardiff–Crewe services and hauling weekend Cambrian line services between Shrewsbury–Aberystwyth/Pwllheli; these latter services were those to/from Birmingham and London Euston. The locomotives also found use on services from Cardiff to Liverpool/Manchester but when the locomotive-hauled services were replaced by multiple unit trainsets, the locomotives were moved to England where they were distributed between the freight sectors that had been established during the 1980s.

(Image 85): 37427 *Bont Y Bermo* bears original Large Logo Corporate Blue livery as it curves out of Ludlow on 24 September 1990 while working a Liverpool Lime St–Cardiff service.

(Image 86): 37426 *Y Lein Fach/Vale of Rheidol* bears original Large Logo Corporate Blue livery as it climbs out of Barmouth on 23 May 1987 while working a Pwllheli–Euston dated service.

(Image 87): The signalman exchanges tokens at Towyn/Twywn on 14 June 1986 as 37428 + 37430 *Cwmbran*, both bearing Large Logo Corporate Blue livery, call while working a Pwllheli–Birmingham New St dated service.

(Image 88): 37428 *David Lloyd George* bears original Large Logo Corporate Blue livery as it powers out of Liverpool Lime St on 27 July 1987 while working a Liverpool Lime St–Cardiff service.

3.2: NORTH WALES COAST

The first appearance of Class 37/4 traction on the North Wales Coast line came in 1993 when, as part of the Club Train diagram (see **Section 2.1**), the Southport trainset was used to work a Manchester–Holyhead service that connected with the Irish boat service. When the Club Train workings were discontinued the locomotives and trainsets, based at Crewe, were transferred to work services from Crewe along the North Wales Coast. These continued until January 2001 when the timetables were recast by First North Western as a prelude to handing over services to create a new Welsh-based franchise that was awarded to Arriva Trains in 2003.

Above (Image 89): 37412 *Driver George Elliot* bears Transrail Freight livery and branding as it speeds past Llanfairfechan on 30 August 1999 while working a Holyhead–Crewe service.

Left (Image 90): 37418 *East Lancashire Railway* bears Regional Railways livery and branding as it passes Mostyn Dock on 27 July 1996 while working a Holyhead–Stockport service.

Right (Image 91): 37414 *Cathays C&W Works 1846-1993* bears Regional Railways livery and branding as it approaches Abergele and Pensarn on 31 March 1997 while working a Crewe–Holyhead service.

Below (Image 92): 37402 *Bont Y Bermo* bears de-branded Railfreight livery as it approaches Mostyn on 12 July 1996 while working a Crewe–Holyhead service. In the background *TSS Duke of Lancaster* lies at rest pending a decision as to its future. Once a railway-owned ferry servicing the Heysham–Belfast route until the service was withdrawn in April 1995, it then became a relief vessel for the Holyhead–Dun Laoghaire route until November 1978 after which it was laid up until moving to Mostyn Dock in August 1979 to become a leisure centre. The intended project was contested by local councils and the owners dropped the project in 2004, since when the vessel has deteriorated further.

(Image 93): 37420 *The Scottish Hosteller* bears Provincial Railways Mainline livery as it passes Mostyn on 20 May 1995 while working a Holyhead–Crewe service.

(Image 94): 37422 *Robert F Fairlie* bears Regional Railways livery and branding as it passes Mostyn on 27 July 1996 while working a Holyhead–Crewe service.

(Image 95): 37417 *Highland Region* bears de-branded Railfreight two-tone Grey livery as it speeds past Greenside on 3 August 1996 while working a Crewe–Bangor service.

Right (Image 96): 37415 bears EWSR livery and branding as it approaches Abergele and Pensarn on 20 June 1999 while working a Birmingham New St–Holyhead service.

Below (Image 97): 37420 *The Scottish Hosteller* bears Provincial Railways Mainline livery as it passes Hargreave on 20 May 1995 while working a Crewe–Chester service.

(Image 98): 37420 *The Scottish Hosteller* bears Regional Railways livery and branding as it approaches Mostyn Dock on 27 July 1996 while working a Bangor–Crewe service.

(Image 99): 37418 *East Lancashire Railway* bears initial EWSR livery and branding albeit devoid of cabside logo as it approaches Abergele and Pensarn on 31 March 1997 while working a Holyhead–Crewe service.

(Image 100): 37420 *The Scottish Hosteller* bears Regional Railways livery and branding as it approaches Mostyn on 27 July 1996 while working a Crewe–Holyhead service. In the background *TSS Duke of Lancaster* deteriorates as arguments rage over its future use.

(Image 101): 37420 *The Scottish Hosteller* speeds through Winwick on 10 May 1997 while working a Stockport–Holyhead service.

(Image 102): 37429 *Eisteddfod Genedlaethol* bears Regional Railways livery and branding as it approaches Prestatyn on 3 August 1996 while working a Stockport–Holyhead service.

(Image 103): 37421 *The Kingsman* bears Regional Railways livery and branding as it curves through Conway Castle on 1 April 1994 while working a Holyhead–Manchester Victoria service that would next form the Manchester Victoria–Southport Club Train service.

(Image 104): 37429 *Eisteddfod Genedlaethol* bears Regional Railways livery and branding as it curves through Conway Castle on 1 April 1994 while working a Holyhead–Crewe service.

(Image 105): 37425 *Sir Robert McAlpine/Concrete Bob* bears Regional Railways livery and branding as it speeds through Abergele and Pensarn on 31 March 1997 while working a Crewe–Bangor service.

(Image 106): 37425 *Sir Robert McAlpine/Concrete Bob* bears Railfreight Construction sector livery and branding as it approaches Mostyn on 20 May 1995 while working a Crewe–Bangor service.

Opposite above (Image 107): 37417 *Highland Region* bears de-branded Railfreight two-tone Grey livery as it speeds past Dwygyfylchi on 2 September 1995 while working a Crewe–Bangor service.

Opposite below (Image 108): 37426 bears EWSR livery and branding as it speeds through Abergele and Pensarn on 3 May 1999 while working a Stockport–Holyhead service.

Above (Image 109): 37422 *Robert F Fairlie* bears Regional Railways livery and branding as it climbs Conway Causeway on 3 May 1999 while working a Birmingham New St–Holyhead service.

3.3: RHYMNEY VALLEY

Among the franchised services when BR was privatised from 1 April 1994, that for the Welsh Valley routes emanating from Cardiff was awarded to the Cardiff Railway Company whose managing director was Tom Clift. He quickly appreciated the value of locomotive-hauled trains for weekday peak hour services and identified the Cardiff–Rhymney service as the best line on which to operate them.

The service initially used privately-owned locomotives with main line certification but Tom Clift soon turned to Class 37/4 locomotives hired from EWSR; a contract that continued through a number of franchise changes. When I made my first visit in 2004, the services were operated by Arriva Trains Wales for which a pool of three dedicated locomotives was allocated to Margam but kept at Rhymney to work both peak hour weekday services and all services between Rhymney and Cardiff on a Saturday.

I made five visits to the Rhymney Valley, including the final weekend in December 2005 when a 'Farewell' timetable was operated that included, in addition to the three dedicated Class 37/4 locomotives, examples of locomotive classes that had operated services since its original inception. The final trains ran to Cardiff on Monday 5 December 2005 when the three Class 37/4 locomotives worked their morning peak hour services and were replaced by multiple unit trainsets for the evening peak hour return services to Rhymney.

My first visit to the Rhymney Valley was on Saturday 28 February 2004 when I stopped off after completing a photography commission in the area. Being a Saturday, all line services between Cardiff and Rhymney were powered by Class 37/4 with three locomotives in use: 37402 *Bont Y Bermo* bearing de-branded Railfreight two-tone Grey livery, 37406 *The Saltire Society*, and 37425 both bearing EWSR livery and branding.

(Image 110): 37406 *The Saltire Society* eases out of Pontlottyn while working a Rhymney–Cardiff service.

Right (Image 111): 37402 *Bont Y Bermo* curves out of Bargoed while working a Cardiff–Rhymney service.

Below (Image 112): 37425 curves into Rhymney with a Cardiff–Rhymney service.

A photographic assignment in South Wales in September 2004 allowed a second visit to Rhymney when the locomotive pool comprised 37402 *Bont Y Bermo* bearing de-branded Railfreight two-tone Grey livery, 37417 *Richard Trevithick* and 37422 *Cardiff Canton*, both bearing EWSR livery and branding. There was an additional weekday service operated by the pool as one morning peak hour service from Cardiff was extended to form a round trip to Fishguard Harbour before returning from Cardiff with an evening peak hour service to Rhymney.

Left (Image 113): 37422 *Cardiff Canton* curves into Tir-phil on 4 September 2004 while working a Cardiff–Rhymney service.

Below (Image 114): 37417 *Richard Trevithick* awaits departure from Fishguard Harbour on 3 September 2004 to Cardiff, where it will continue to Rhymney on an evening peak hour service.

Right (Image 115):
37417 *Richard Trevithick* curves out of Rhymney on 4 September 2004 while working a Rhymney–Cardiff service.

Below (Image 116):
37402 *Bont Y Bermo* approaches Gilfach on 3 September 2004 while working an evening Cardiff–Rhymney peak hour service.

A photography assignment in South Wales in May 2005 was completed by a visit to the Rhymney Valley when the pool comprised 37405 and 37408 *Loch Rannoch* bearing EWSR livery and branding and 37411, which had been restored to original BR Unlined Green livery with small yellow panel.

Left (Image 117): 37408 *Loch Rannoch* climbs to Pontlottyn on 20 May 2005 while working a Cardiff–Rhymney evening peak hour service.

Below (Image 118): 37405 curves out of Rhymney on 21 May 2005 while working a Rhymney–Cardiff service.

(Image 119): 37411 climbs to Pontlottyn on 20 May 2005 while working a Cardiff–Rhymney evening peak hour service.

(Image 120): 37411 curves into Rhymney on 21 May 2005 while working a Cardiff–Rhymney service.

(Image 121): 37425 crosses Bargoed Viaduct on 7 July 2005 while working the first morning Rhymney–Cardiff peak hour service.

(Image 122): 05:30 at Rhymney on 7 July 2005 sees 37405 and 37408 *Loch Rannoch* stabled awaiting their turn to work a morning peak hour service to Cardiff.

(Image 123): 37405 climbs toward Gilfach on 6 July 2005 while working an evening Cardiff–Rhymney peak hour service.

(Image 124): 37408 *Loch Rannoch* stables in Rhymney sidings on 5 July 2005 having been failed with brake problems.

(Image 125): 37425 climbs towards Pontlottyn on 4 July 2005 while working an evening Cardiff–Rhymney peak hour service.

The final locomotive-hauled services ran over the weekend of 3/4 December 2005 when the locomotive pool comprised 37411 *Caerphilly Castle/Castell Caerffili*, 37419 bearing EWSR livery and branding, and 37425 *Pride of the Valley/Balchder Y Cymoedd*; 37411 and 37425 had been both repainted and named by Arriva Trains Wales.

The end of locomotive-hauled services was commemorated on Sunday 4 December when a special timetable of Rhymney–Cardiff services was operated and the locomotive pool was expanded by the inclusion of locomotive types which had been used since the inception of locomotive haulage by Tom Clift in the 1990s. The visiting locomotives were Class 33/2 33207 and Class 47/8 47854 kindly supplied by the West Coast Railway Company and Class 50 50031 *Hood* and 50049 *Defiance* kindly provided by the Fifty Fund based on the Severn Valley Railway.

Saturday evening departures from Rhymney to Cardiff on 3 December 2005 included …

Left (Image 126): … 37419.

Below (Image 127): …37425 *Pride of the Valley/Balchder Y Cymoedd.*

Scenes of 'Farewell to locomotive haulage' services on 4 December 2005 at Pontlottyn included …

(Image 128): 37411 *Caerphilly Castle/ Castell Caerffili* departing while working a Rhymney– Cardiff service.

(Image 129): 37419 departing while working a Rhymney– Cardiff service.

(Image 130): 37425 *Pride of the Valley/ Balchder Y Cymoedd* approaching while working a Cardiff– Rhymney service.

Above (Image 131): 37419 approaches Gilfach on 4 December 2005 while working a Rhymney–Cardiff 'Farewell' service.

Opposite above (Image 132): 37411 *Caerphilly Castle/Castell Caerffili* stands in Rhymney on 4 December 2005 after working its final 'Farewell' Cardiff–Rhymney service of the day then

Opposite below (Image 133): ... moved to the sidings for overnight stabling.

The finale came on Monday 5 December when the three locomotives worked their respective morning peak hour services to Cardiff then were replaced by DMU trainsets for the evening return services.

SECTION 4: CHARTER / RAILTOUR SERVICES

When class members were displaced from regular passenger service they were initially allocated to one of the freight sectors created during the 1980s sectorisation programme but, despite the freight activity, the locomotives proved popular with many tour organisers to haul both charter and railtour services.

Left (Image 134): 37401 bears de-branded *Royal Scotsman* livery as it works in top'n tail mode with Class 67 67029 *Royal Diamond* when they curve out of the Ribble Steam Railway base at Riversway onto the Marina Bridge on 19 January 2008 while working the Preston Dock–Heysham leg of Hertfordshire Railtours 'Preston Docker' railtour …

Opposite above (Image 135): … having previously stabled at Riversway while the trainset was serviced and passengers visited the site facilities.

Opposite Below (Image 136): 37416 bears de-branded *Royal Scotsman* livery as it approaches Riversway during a stock shunt on 19 November 2005 after its arrival with Pathfinder Tours' Newport–Preston Dock railtour which it had powered in top 'n tail mode with Class 60 60042 *Hundred of Hoo*.

(Image 137): 37431 *Bullidae* bears Provincial Railways Mainline livery and Petroleum Sector branding under the leading cab window as it curves out of Edge Hill Down Wapping on 13 November 1991 while working an Edge Hill CS–Manchester Victoria stock move prior to working a Footex.

(Image 138): 37403 / D6607 *Ben Cruachan* bears original BR Unlined Green livery with small yellow panel as it stables at Southport on 17 July 1998 while waiting to return to Rugby with a charter operated in conjunction with the Open Golf Championship being held at Hillside Golf Club.

(Image 139): 37416 bears de-branded *Royal Scotsman* livery as it works in top 'n tail mode with Class 60 60042 *Hundred of Hoo* when curving into Rufford on 19 November 2005 while working the Preston–Ormskirk leg of Pathfinder Tours' Newport–Preston Dock railtour.

A railtour ran from Peterborough to Blaenau Ffestiniog on 31 May 2008 hauled by 37417 *Richard Trevithick* + 37401, both bearing EWSR livery and branding; a visit was made to the Conway Valley where the undernoted images were taken.

(Image 140): 37417 *Richard Trevithick* + 37401 power past Bont Y Pant on the outward journey.

(Image 141): 37401 + 37417 *Richard Trevithick* stable at Blaenau Ffestiniog while the trainset is serviced.

(Image 142): 37401 + 37417 *Richard Trevithick* power through Dolwyddelen on the return journey.

Left (Image 143): 37406 *The Saltire Society* bears EWSR livery and branding as it works in top 'n tail mode with 37417 *Richard Trevithick* as they power through Newton-le-Willows on 24 June 2006 while working Pathfinder Tours' Liverpool Lime St–York railtour.

Below (Image 144): 37426 *Y Lein Fach/Vale of Rheidol* bears original Large Logo Corporate Blue livery as it approaches Arnside on 9 April 1998 while working the Barrow–Warrington Bank Quay leg of the Pathfinders Railtours' 'Morecambe Marauder' railtour from Taunton that traversed local lines in the north-west of England.

Right (Image 145): 37430 *Cwmbran* + 37412 *Driver George Elliot,* both bearing Transrail Freight livery and branding, stable at Southport on 25 April 1999 with the stock of a Southport–Edinburgh charter that had run the previous day.

Below (Image 146): 37418 *Pectinidae* bears Railfreight Petroleum sector livery and branding as it crosses Levens Viaduct on 25 April 1992 while working a Preston–Barrow service during the North West Diesel Day when First North Western operated some locomotive-hauled services with freight sector locomotives.

Left (Image 147): 37417 *Richard Trevithick* + 37401, both bearing EWSR livery and branding, curve through Euxton on 14 June 2008 while working the Barrow–Cardiff leg of a Pathfinders Tours' railtour.

Below (Image 148): 37427 bears EWSR livery and branding as it climbs through Leyland on 2 May 2005 while working a Pathfinders Tours' charter returning from Workington to Swindon. Haulage was intended to be a pair of Class 37/4 locomotives but the failure of 37422 en route had caused it to be detached at Preston hence leaving 37427 to continue unassisted.

(Image 149): 37428 *Loch Long/Loch Awe*, bearing *Royal Scotsman* livery ,+ 37427, bearing EWSR livery and branding, stand at Crewe on 31 May 2003 while working the Scottish Railway Preservation Society's Linlithgow–Chester charter.

(Image 150): 37411 *Scottish Railway Preservation Society* + 37405, both bearing EWSR livery and branding, power across Whalley Viaduct on 14 September 2002 while working a Scottish Railway Preservation Society charter from Morpeth to Chester then …

(Image 151): … power through Balshaw Lane Junction on the return journey later in the day.

SECTION 5: FREIGHT SERVICES

When the class members were replaced on passenger services by DMUs, their initial allocation was to one of the freight sectors that had been created in the early 1980s but, on the privatisation of BR on 1 April 1994, all surviving class members were allocated to Transrail Freight. This was one of the three freight companies created on 1 April 1994 and was created to service all freight services in the north of England and Scotland. The freight companies were bought by Wisconsin Central, an American railway company, in February 1996 then melded into a single operation trading as English Welsh and Scottish Railways (EWSR). The company has changed ownership and trading names since that date, hence, as at August 2020, operates as DB Cargo UK – a division of the German state railway Deutsches Bahn (DB).

Above (Image 152): 37416, bearing Provincial Railways Mainline livery, + 37413 *Loch Eil Outward Bound*, bearing Transrail Freight livery, curve through Winwick on 3 September 1995 while working an Irvine–Burngullow china clay service.

Left (Image 153): 37415, bearing Provincial Railways Mainline livery, + 37026 *Shap Fell*, bearing Civil Engineers' Grey livery, join the main line at Chinley North Junction on 5 May 1995 while working a Tunstead–Oakleigh limestone service.

(Image 154): 37418 *Gordon Grigg* bears Railfreight Petroleum sector livery and branding as it curves through Beckfoot on 21 March 1992 while working a Dalston–Stanlow fuel service.

(Image 155): 37420 *The Scottish Hosteller* bears Provincial Railways Mainline livery as it stables in Peak Forest Stabling Point on 17 September 1994 awaiting its next duty.

(Image 156): 37405 *Strathclyde Region*, bearing Provincial Railways Mainline livery, + 37116 *Sister Dora*, bearing Mainline Freight livery and branding, stable at Ainsdale on 9 February 1997 with an engineer's train.

(Image 157): 37421 *Strombinidae* bears Railfreight Petroleum sector livery and branding as it awaits departure from Aberystwyth on 27 May 1992 while working a fuel service to Stanlow.

(Image 158): 37429 *Eisteddfod Genedlaethol* + 37214, both bearing Railfreight Construction livery and branding, curve through Beckfoot on 27 March 1995 while working a Clitheroe–Gunnie cement service.

(Image 159): 37425 *Pride of the Valley/Balchder Cymoedd,* bearing Large Logo Corporate Blue livery + 37411 *Caerphilly Castle/ Castell Caerffili*, bearing BR Unlined Green livery, pass Euxton on 15 October 2007 while working the Blackburn–Arpley local trip service.

(Image 160): 37407 *Blackpool Tower* bears Transrail Freight livery and branding as it curves through Winwick on 22 October 1997 while working an Arpley–Ince Moss engineers' spoil train.

(Image 161): 37423 *Sir Murray Morrison 1873-1948 Pioneer of the British Aluminium Industry* bears Railfreight Metals/Automotive sector livery and branding as it stables in Fort William depot on 28 August 1988.

(Image 162): 37429 *Eisteddfod Genedlaethol* bears Regional Railways livery and branding as it passes Balshaw Lane Junction on 22 April 1999 while working a Cardiff–Mossend 'Enterprise' service.

The first English Welsh Scottish Railway branding included the text 'EW&S' which was only applied to 37 415 / 418 / 419 / 427 before being modified to 'EWS'; scenes of 37415 bearing the initial branding include it …

Left (Image 163): … posing at Preston Strand Road crossing on 12 March 2003 when Healey Mills drivers were route-learning before the resumption of the Lindsey Oil Refinery–Preston Docks bitumen service.

Below (Image 164): … curving through Leyland on 2 July 2002 while working an Arpley–Carnforth Civil Engineer's service.

(Image 165): 37427 propels Class 86/2 86244 *The Royal British Legion* into a bay platform at Preston on 5 June 2001 after rescuing the failed electric locomotive and its Glasgow Central–Euston service.

(Image 166): 37401 drifts past Buxworth on 4 March 2008 while working a Dowlow–Arpley limestone service.

A regular working for Class 37/4 locomotives was a weekday trip working from Arpley Sidings to Blackburn and return; scenes of the Blackburn–Arpley leg include …

(Image 167): … 37401 + Class 37/5 37670 *St Blazey T&RSMD* passing Balshaw Lane Junction on 20 May 2009.

(Image 168): … 37401 passing Balshaw Lane Junction on 25 November 2009.

(Image 169): … 37417 *Richard Trevithick* passing Balshaw Lane Junction on 4 June 2008.

(Image 170): ... 37405 curving through Winwick on 3 March 2008.

(Image 171): ... 37417 *Richard Trevithick* passing Euxton on 22 October 2008.

(Image 172): 37422 *Cardiff Canton* curves through Leyland on 16 July 2008 while working the Arpley–Blackburn leg of the daily working.

(Image 173): 37401 eases through Portway on 26 June 2008 while working a Burton Steel Terminal–Bescot steel train.

(Image 174): 37422 *Cardiff Canton* + 37410 approach Hebden Bridge on 9 August 2007 while working a Crewe Basford Hall–Scunthorpe engineers' service and …

(Image 175): … sees 37410 at the rear of the pairing as they pass through the staggered platforms of the station.

(Image 176): 37426 eases through Winwick on 22 May 2001 while working an Arpley–Deanside container service; this was a trial working that only lasted a short period.

(Image 177): 37422 stables in Eastleigh Works during the works' Centenary Open Weekend on 25 May 2009. The locomotive was awaiting attention as a prelude to being sold to Direct Rail Services (DRS) (see **Section 6.6**).

(Image 178): 37428 *Loch Long/Loch Awe*, freshly painted in *Royal Scotsman* livery, curves through Carnforth on 8 April 2003 while working a Carnforth–Crewe Basford Hall Civil Engineers' service.

SECTION 6: DIRECT RAIL SERVICES (DRS)

DRS began operating in 1994, as a consequence of the privatisation of British Rail, to provide dedicated transport to the nuclear industry geared to the transport of nuclear material to/from the Sellafield nuclear facility on the Furness coast. The operation began with the purchase of Class 20 and Class 37 locomotives made surplus by the freight sectors but, as the company increased its customer base, it purchased Class 66 locomotives to service the new contracts.

Its first purchase of a Class 37/4 locomotive was that of 37423 which was bought ostensibly to haul nuclear flasks; it was sent to Brush Traction at Loughborough for overhaul and entered service with DRS in September 2007. The company then bought 37409 / 412 in 2008 while in 2010 DB Schenker withdrew the 37/4 fleet from service and offered the survivors for sale. DRS bought all locomotives – some for traffic and some for spares, hence as at 1 January 2014 its operational fleet comprised 37401 / 402 / 405 / 409 / 422 / 423 / 425. Demand for Class 37/4 locomotives subsequently led DRS during 2015 to hire preserved 37403 from the Scottish Railway Preservation Society at Bo'ness and buy preserved 37407 / 427 from their private owner based on the Churnet Valley Railway (CVR).

DRS has found their Class 37/4 fleet to be a useful asset which has allowed the company to successfully tender for short term passenger contracts, infrastructure service for Network Rail, and provide traction for a variety of charters/railtours.

6.1: CUMBRIAN FLOODEX

In November 2009 a violent storm hit the Furness Coast and destroyed the road link to the north of Workington, thus leaving rail transport as the only link with locations north of the town. The government commissioned DRS to provide an hourly service between Workington and Maryport using a rake of four coaches worked in top 'n tail mode by a pair of locomotives. The service began on 30 November 2009 and continued operating until 2 May 2010.

My first visit was made on the 2nd day of the temporary service, 1 December 2009, when services were powered by 37423 *Spirit of the Lakes* working in top 'n tail mode with Class 47/7 47790 *Galloway Princess*, and found that travel on the service was free as the government was meeting the full cost of the service. I made further visits during the 6-month operation of the service and found that traction was provided by examples of Classes 37/6, 47/4, 47/7, 47/8 and 57/0; 37423 *Spirit of the Lakes* appeared to have been used only for a couple of days during the first week of operation.

Left (Image 179): 37423 *Spirit of the Lakes*, working in top 'n tail mode with Class 47/7 47790 *Galloway Princess*, curves past Siddick Wind Farm while working the 11:20 Workington–Maryport service.

Opposite above (Image 180): 37423 *Spirit of the Lakes* arrives at Maryport with the first service of the day from Workington.

Opposite below (Image 181): 37423 *Spirit of the Lakes* awaits departure from Workington with the 08:10 service to Maryport.

(Image 182): 37423 *Spirit of the Lakes* stables at Maryport after its arrival with the 08:10 service from Workington.

(Image 183): 37423 *Spirit of the Lakes* works in top 'n tail mode with Class 47/7 47790 *Galloway Princess* as they curve into Maryport while working the 12:20 Workington–Maryport service.

6.2: CUMBRIAN COAST SERVICES

In May 2015 DRS began operating a number of Carlisle–Barrow services on behalf of Northern Trains with Class 37 haulage, initially worked as top 'n tail services, with at least one locomotive being a Class 37/4 example. The later receipt of driving trailers, originally modified for use on Edinburgh–Glasgow services in the 1970s, saw workings being operated with Class 37/4 and driving trailer combinations.

The timetable also provided that the weekday 05:15 Carlisle–Barrow service was extended to Preston while a Saturday afternoon Carlisle–Barrow service was extended to Lancaster. The service continued until December 2018 and its cessation was marked with a Carlisle–Barrow–Carnforth 'Farewell' working on 11 January 2019.

(Image 184): 37401 *Mary Queen of Scots,* bearing ScotRail Corporate Blue livery with West Highland Terrier Logo, works in top 'n tail mode with 37409 *Lord Hinton* as they approach Brock on 6 August 2015 while working the weekday Carlisle–Barrow–Preston service.

(Image 185): 37402 *Stephen Middlemore 23.12.1954-8.6.2013* bears ScotRail Corporate Blue livery with West Highland Terrier logo, as it approaches Brock on 4 May 2017 while working the weekday Preston–Barrow service.

(Image 186): 37409 *Lord Hinton* works in top 'n tail mode with 37419 *Carl Havilland 1954-2012* as they approach Brock on 20 May 2015 while working the weekday Preston–Barrow service.

(Image 187): 37402 *Stephen Middlemore 23.12.1954-8.6.2013* bears ScotRail Corporate Blue livery with West Highland Terrier logo, as it approaches Brock on 19 October 2016 while working the weekday Preston–Barrow service.

Above (Image 188): 37402 *Stephen Middlemore 23.12.1954 - 8.6.2013* works in top 'n tail mode with Class 37/0 37218 as they approach Brock on 16 June 2015 while working the weekday Carlisle–Barrow–Preston service.

Right (Image 189): 37409 *Lord Hinton* works in top 'n tail mode with Class 37/0 37218 on 10 July 2015 as they approach Brock while working the weekday Carlisle–Barrow–Preston service.

Below (Image 190): 37419 *Carl Havilland 1954-2012* works in top 'n tail mode with 37409 *Lord Hinton* as they approach Brock on 20 May 2015 while working the weekday Carlisle–Barrow–Preston service.

Left (Image 191): 37402 *Stephen Middlemore 23.12.1954 - 8.6.2013* bears ScotRail Corporate Blue livery with West Highland Terrier Logo as it awaits departure from Preston on 23 November 2016 while working the weekday Preston–Barrow service.

Below (Image 192): 37403 *Isle of Mull* bears ScotRail Corporate Blue livery with West Highland Terrier Logo as it approaches Brock on 5 August 2016 while working the weekday Preston–Barrow service.

Above (Image 193): 37425 *Sir Robert McAlpine/Concrete Bob* passes Bay Horse on 14 December 2016 while propelling the weekday Carlisle–Barrow–Preston service.

Right (Image 194): 37409 *Lord Hinton* propels the weekday Carlisle–Barrow–Preston service through Bay Horse on 5 August 2016.

Below (Image 195): 37402 *Stephen Middlemore 23.12.1954 - 8.6.2013* bears ScotRail Corporate Blue livery with West Highland Terrier Logo as it passes Bay Horse on 16 November 2016 while propelling the weekday Carlisle–Barrow–Preston service.

(Image 196): 37409 *Lord Hinton* curves through Bay Horse on 9 November 2016 while working the weekday Preston–Barrow service.

(Image 197): 37402 *Stephen Middlemore 23.12.1954-8.6.2013* bears ScotRail Corporate Blue livery with West Highland Terrier Logo as it curves through Bay Horse on 28 November 2016 while working the weekday Preston–Barrow service.

Right (Image 198): Dawn breaks over Carlisle on 17 July 2015 as 37409 *Lord Hinton* awaits departure with the weekday 05:15 Carlisle–Barrow–Preston service.

Below (Image 199): 37401 *Mary Queen of Scots* bears ScotRail Corporate Blue livery with West Highland Terrier Logo as it stands at Preston on 29 June 2016 after its arrival while working the weekday Carlisle–Barrow–Preston service.

Left (Image 200): 37423 *Spirit of the Lakes* works in top 'n tail mode with Class 37/0 37259 as they weave into Carnforth on 17 February 2016 while working the weekday Preston–Barrow service.

Below (Image 201): 37409 *Lord Hinton* weaves into Carnforth on 18 March 2016 with a Lancaster–Barrow stock move following failure of the trainset and cancellation of its weekday Preston–Barrow service.

(Image 202): 37403 *Isle of Mull* bears ScotRail Corporate Blue livery with West Highland Terrier Logo as it propels the Saturday Carlisle–Barrow–Lancaster service into Arnside on 24 March 2018.

(Image 203): 37403 *Isle of Mull* bears ScotRail Corporate Blue livery with West Highland Terrier Logo as it departs from Arnside on 29 October 2016 while propelling the Saturday Carlisle–Barrow–Lancaster service …

(Image 204): … then departs later in the day while working the return Lancaster–Barrow service.

(Image 205): 37401 *Mary Queen of Scots* bears ScotRail Corporate Blue livery with West Highland Terrier logo as it works in top 'n tail mode with 37402 *Stephen Middlemore 23.12.1954 - 8.6.2013* as they approach Arnside on 8 August 2015 while working the Saturday Carlisle–Barrow–Lancaster service.

(Image 206): 37409 *Lord Hinton* works in top 'n tail mode with Class 37/5 37688 *Kingmoor TMD* as they enter Arnside on 6 June 2015 while working the Saturday Carlisle–Barrow–Lancaster service.

Above (Image 207) / Below (Image 208): 37401 *Mary Queen of Scots,* bearing Large Logo Corporate Blue livery, forms the rear of the Saturday Lancaster–Barrow service led by 37402 *Stephen Middlemore 23.12.1954 - 8.6.2013* as they depart from Arnside on 8 August 2015 and cross the Kent estuary.

(Image 209): 37422 bears base blue livery as it propels the Saturday Carlisle–Barrow–Lancaster service out of Arnside on 20 August 2016.

(Image 210): A 'Farewell to Furness Coast Class 37s' railtour ran on 11 January 2019 from Carlisle to Carnforth via Barrow with the fares being donated to charity. The return journey was photographed at Arnside as 37409 *Lord Hinton,* bearing Large Logo Corporate Blue livery, formed the rear of a consist led by 37425 *Sir Robert McAlpine/Concrete Bob.*

6.3: CHARTER WORKINGS

Members of the Class 37/4 fleet have always been popular traction for charter work, especially for enthusiast railtours, and the transfer of the remaining Class 37/4 locomotives to DRS has not diminished that demand. As at August 2020, DRS is one of only two operators of Class 37/4 traction on the main line hence the use of its Class 37/4 fleet on charters/railtours.

(Image 211): 37402 *Stephen Middlemore 23.12.1954 - 8.6.2013* pilots Class 37/6 37604 as they speed through Balshaw Lane Junction on 9 July 2014 while working a Pathfinder Tours' Taunton–Carlisle railtour.

(Image 212): The Friends of the Settle & Carlisle Line (FoSCL) organised a charter on 11 April 2014 to celebrate the 25th Anniversary of the rescinding of the proposed Settle & Carlisle closure. The charter was operated by DRS using Class 37 locomotives and was photographed at Ribblehead Viaduct where Class 37/0 37259 was noted pilotting 37425 *Sir Robert McAlpine/Concrete Bob* with 37409 *Lord Hinton* providing rear end assistance as the consist curved off the viaduct while working the Carlisle–Leeds leg of the charter.

Above (Image 213): 37423 climbs through Euxton on 20 June 2008 while hauling a stock move from Carnforth (WCRC) to Crewe prior to working a railtour the following day.

Opposite (Image 214): 37419 *Carl Havilland 1954 - 2012* works in top 'n tail mode with Class 37/6 37604 as they amble past Meadow Lane on 7 March 2015 on the approach to Burscough Junction while working the Preston–Ormskirk–Preston Dock leg of Pathfinder Tours' 'The Lancs Link' railtour that had originated from Crewe.

6.4: HERITAGE CENTRES

DRS has occasionally provided locomotives to heritage lines and the Class 37/4s have proved a popular addition to the pool of locomotives that are made available.

The Ribble Steam Railway hosted 37424 *Avro Vulcan XH558*, bearing Large Logo Corporate Blue livery, over the weekend of 30 September/1 November 2017 as this locomotive had become a particular favourite for heritage line events. When released to service after purchase from preservation and receiving major overhaul, the locomotive was dedicated to the preserved Vulcan bomber XH 558 by carrying both the nameplate *Avro Vulcan XH558* and bodyside number 37558 despite being officially recorded as 37424.

Left (Image 215): 37424 *Avro Vulcan XH558* forms the rear of a Riversway–Strand Road crossing shuttle service on 30 September 2017.

Opposite above (Image 216): 37424 *Avro Vulcan XH558* curves away from Riversway Walk on 30 September 2017 while working a Strand Road crossing–Riversway shuttle in top 'n tail mode with Class 14 D9539 + Class 03 D2148.

Opposite below (Image 217): 37424 *Avro Vulcan XH558* rests on shed during a lunch break on 30 September 2017.

(Image 218): The nameplate and bodyside number applied to 37424.

(Image 219): 37419 poses in the National Rail Museum's York yard on 5 June 2012 while appearing as a display item at the NRM's RailFest 2012 event.

6.5: NETWORK RAIL SERVICES

DRS is a regular supplier of traction to Network Rail, in addition to companies such as Colas Rail, DB Cargo UK and Freightliner which also supply locomotives. DRS, however, has a large selection of Class 37 locomotives, hence the use of Class 37/4 locomotives on a variety of services.

(Image 220): 37425 enters Carlisle in the early hours of 16 November 2012 while working the Mossend–Carlisle leg of a Network Rail inspection service.

(Image 221): 37423 *Spirit of the Lakes* works in top 'n tail mode with 37407 *Blackpool Tower* as they speed through Bamber Bridge on 19 June 2020 while working the Blackpool North–Derby RTC leg of a regular Network Rail inspection service …

(Image 222): … with 37407 *Blackpool Tower* bearing Large Logo Corporate Blue livery as it provides rear end assistance.

Above left (Image 223): 37423 *Spirit of the Lakes* stables at York on 4 April 2012 with Network Rail's inspection coach ADB 975025 *Caroline*.

Above right (Image 224): 37423 *Spirit of the Lakes* propels Network Rail inspection coach ADB 975025 *Caroline* through Portway on 2 July 2009 while en route from Gloucester to their base at Derby RTC.

6.6: TRANSFERS

With bases at both Crewe Gresty Bridge and Carlisle Kingmoor, there are frequent transfers between the two centres, as noted below.

Above (Image 225): 37402 *Stephen Middlemore 23.12.1954 - 8.6.2013* + Class 66/4 66433 drift through Euxton on 12 June 2014 while transferring from Carlisle Kingmoor to Crewe Gresty Bridge.

Opposite above (Image 226): 37422 bears base blue livery as it is tested after major overhaul at Crewe, hence its appearance at Winwick on 12 August 2015 while undertaking a Crewe Gresty Bridge–Preston test run with Class 57/0 57004 being provided as insurance in case of failure.

Opposite below (Image 227): A triple transfer from Crewe Gresty Bridge–Carlisle Kingmoor passes Balshaw Lane Junction on 10 June 2019 comprising Class 68 68015, Class 37/4 37419 *Carl Haviland 1954 - 2012* freshly re-liveried in Provincial Railways Mainline livery and Class 68 68002 *Intrepid*.

SECTION 7: COLAS RAIL

Colas Rail gained contracts for Network Rail services that led to the company obtaining Class 37 locomotives including 2 Class 37/4 examples – 37418 *East Lancashire Railway* hired from a private owner based on the East Lancashire Railway and 37421 which was bought from a private owner based at the Pontypool & Blaenavon Railway.

(Image 228): 37421 is at the rear of a Blackpool North–Derby RTC Network Rail inspection train as it passes Lostock Hall Junction on 21 April 2017 led by Class 37/0 37057.

(Image 229): 37421 works in top 'n tail mode with Class 37/0 37219 *Jonty Jarvis 8-12-1998 to 18-3-2005* as they curve through Lostock Hall on 1 December 2017 while working a Carnforth–Derby RTC Network Rail inspection train.

(Image 230): 37421 works in top 'n tail mode with Class 37/0 37219 *Jonty Jarvis 8-12-1998 to 18-3-2005* as they speed through Balshaw Lane Junction on 18 October 2016 while working a Derby RTC–Mossend Network Rail inspection train.

SECTION 8: PRESERVATION

The Class 37 locomotives have proved a popular buy for heritage lines when the opportunity arises, hence the number of withdrawn Class 37/4 locomotives that entered preservation when offered for sale. Some of the preserved examples were subsequently bought or hired by companies which entered the field of railway operation as a result of the privatisation of British Rail in 1994 thus confirming the value of the design almost sixty years after the class first entered service with BR in 1961.

Left (Image 231): 37407 stables at Cheddleton (Churnet Valley Railway) on 6 June 2012 awaiting restoration.

Below (Image 232): 37407 is noted with a coating of protective paint at Cheddleton on 8 February 2014. This locomotive was subsequently sold to DRS in April 2015 and restored to traffic as 37407 *Blackpool Tower* bearing Large Logo Corporate Blue livery.

(Image 233): 37424 stables at Cheddleton (Churnet Valley Railway) on 6 June 2012 awaiting restoration.

(Image 234): 37424 is noted with a coating of protective paint at Cheddleton on 8 February 2014. This locomotive was subsequently sold to DRS in April 2015 and restored to traffic as 37424 *Avro Vulcan XH558* bearing Large Logo Corporate Blue livery.

Opposite above (Image 235): 37403 / D6607 stands in Bo'ness (Bo'ness & Kinneil Railway) on 23 February 2009 awaiting restoration. Once restored as 37403 *Isle of Mull*, this locomotive was subsequently hired by DRS from January 2016 until July 2020 (see **Section 6.2**)

Opposite below (Image 236): 37413 stands in Bo'ness (Bo'ness & Kinneil Railway) on 23 February 2009 to provide a source of spares for the restoration of resident Class 37 locomotives.

Above (Image 237): 37409 lies in storage at Harry Needles' storage yard at Barrow Hill on 4 April 2009; this locomotive had been sold to DRS in September 2008 by whom it was restored to traffic as 37409 *Lord Hinton*.

37418 entered preservation on the East Lancashire Railway in March 2009 and was restored to working order. The loco was hired to Colas Rail in January 2019 and from June 2019 thru March 2020 was allocated to passenger duty on Rhymney Valley services; as at August 2020 it remains on hire to Colas Rail.

Left (Image 238): 37418 *Pectinidae*, bearing EWSR livery and branding, works in top 'n tail mode with Class 37/0 37109 as they pass Radcliffe (on the Metrolink network) on 6 February 2010 while working a Buckley Wells–Whitfield engineering train on behalf of Metrolink.

Below (Image 239): 37418 *Pectinidae* bears EWSR livery and branding as it forms the rear of a Heywood–Rawtenstall service hauled by Class 40 40145 *East Lancashire Railway* when they call at Irwell Vale on 9 January 2010.

Opposite above (Image 240): 37418 bears unbranded Corporate Blue livery as it powers past Townsend Fold on 4 July 2015 while working a Heywood–Rawtenstall service.

Opposite below (Image 241): 37418 curves into Ramsbottom on 4 July 2015 while working a Rawtenstall–Heywood service.

(**Image 242**): 37403 *Isle of Mull,* bearing ScotRail Corporate Blue livery with West Highland Terrier Logo, heads into the sunset at Arnside on 24 March 2018 as it crosses the Kent estuary while working the Saturday Lancaster–Barrow loco-hauled service.